40 Coupons for the best Mum in the world

I bought these coupons to show you how much you mean they are full of fun activities we can do together, & task do for you to make your life a little bit easier.

Use these coupons at any time & in any order, redeem one a week? One a month? The choice is yours.

Simply cut the coupon out and hand it to the gift giver to redeem.

20 Lovely prompted coupons & 20 blank coupons.

Use the blank coupons however you desire.

The gift giver can also fill in some blank coupons that cater to your specific situation & needs.

I hope you enjoy.

Copyright Protected, All Rights Reserved
No part of this publication may be reproduced,stored,copied or shared by any means,
electronic or physical, or used in any manner without the prior written consent of the publisher.

Enjoy!

Gifted to: _____

From: _____

Occasion: _____

Enjoy!

One home afternoon tea experience.
(Including scones & jam, sandwiches, sweet treats & unlimited tea)

Enjoy!

One Duvet day.
(Have a lazy day together watching movies,
do as little as possible)

Enjoy!

One day of unlimited tea or
coffee for you.
(I will make you a cuppa whenever you ask)

Enjoy!

One chauffeur service.

(I will drive you anywhere you want to go)

Enjoy!

One family game night.
(I will organise the games, food & drinks)

Enjoy!

One relaxing bath with candles,
bubbles & no interuptions.
(I will prepare this for you)

Enjoy!

Surprise hamper.
(Go to the shop and pick an assortment of goodies
that your mum would like, eg; snacks, drinks, new
book,etc)

Enjoy!

One baking afternoon.
(Spend an afternoon together baking something yummy, Mum chooses the recipe)

Enjoy!

Breakfast in bed.

(whatever you request)

Enjoy!

One home spa evening.
(treat your mum to a relaxing evening. Arrange face masks, cucumber slices, skincare set, essential oils, spa music, dim lighting)

Enjoy!

Cheese & wine night together.
(Buy an assortment of cheese & alcohol, spend the
night chilling out)

Enjoy!

Takeaway surprise.
(Order a takeaway that neither of you has tried before)

Enjoy!

A trip away together.
(Plan a little adventure or trip away together,
make it happen within the next year)

Enjoy!

One themed evening for the family.
(Decide on a theme together and make it happen, eg;
Mexico. Think nachos, fajitas, tequila, Mexican music &
even fancy dress)

Enjoy!

No phones allowed.
(Everyone in the house must put their phones in a drawer, enjoy dinner & the evening together with no distractions)

Enjoy!

An afternoon of fun.
(Spend an afternoon together enjoying your mum's favourite hobbies. Gardening? Reading? A long walk? Baking?)

Enjoy!

Mum's the DJ.
(Spend the evening together listening to Mum's favourite music)

Enjoy!

A stroll down memory lane.
(Spend some time looking through old family photos together)

Enjoy!

Home cocktail party.
(Find cocktail recipes online & spend an evening
making & drinking various concoctions together)

Enjoy!

Enjoy!

Enjoy!

Enjoy!

Enjoy!

Enjoy!

Enjoy!

Enjoy!

Enjoy!

Enjoy!

Enjoy!

Enjoy!

Enjoy!

Enjoy!

Enjoy!

Enjoy!

Enjoy!

Enjoy!

Enjoy!

Enjoy!

Printed in Great Britain
by Amazon

58308697R00047